SYNCHRONIZATION OF DIMENSIONS

By Sosé Gjelaj and Elitsa Teneva

Copyright © 2016

All Rights Reserved

Sovereignterra.com
Powerfulstructures.com
Soseartgallery.com

ELITSA: What is your opinion on laws created within the scope of the legal system?

SOSÉ: *Law officials tend not to look at life in different perspectives as doing so would translate into finding solutions to the problems that we face. They rather look away as they are focused on one thought only – profit. Law officials become entangled in the world of materialistic power, which imprisons and drains the spirit, the true soul, the essence of Godliness. In order to protect the illusion, they formulate laws outside of the pure heart. The more laws being formulated on the planet under such conditions, the more of the thieves emerge. Legal bureaucracy arises as a result of the desire for ownership. In a heart full of love, human-created laws do not exist.*

ELITSA: Legal enforcement works on the basis of punishing noncompliance while rewarding compliance with the law. Does forcing compliance contribute to positive outcomes? How are people affected by such a conduct psychologically? Is it taking away their innate ability to discern between right and wrong? Is it instilling fear?

SOSÉ: *Laws are relative principles, creating devotional supreme personality. It is a sacrificial action preventing the spirit to be consciously present. When false ego presents itself, it creates perceptions and identities leading to spiritual detachments.*

The only purpose of laws is to create fear (from punishment and social ostracizing) and confusion in our consciousness, to exert control over the human psyche as a means of acquiring profit and resulting power. Laws were intentionally designed to focus on our shortcomings, not on our strengths, philanthropy and human grandness. The more we were made to feel guilty through legal means, the more we felt that we had shortcomings and the more we supported the legal systems financially and otherwise. We gave with our beautiful hearts. We trusted that it was in the proper hands, which it was not. More organizations were launched to modify the behavior of human beings, not to heal them. Ultimately, in order to remove the extravagance, we need to remove the ignorance through questioning the truth and taking solution-oriented actions. The solution is in the absence of false ego.

ELITSA: How do laws affect us and change our essence from being Godly, divine beings to being transhuman entities?

SOSÉ: We are infinite potential. Conditioning creates separation. Governments feared our infinite divinity, created laws to imprison the expression of our beauty thus continuing to generate profit and remain in power. Governments fear us. It is not the other way around. Without our support, they would lose complete control over humanity and Earth.

ELITSA: Are elections rigged?

SOSÉ: Isn't it our responsibility to question that if we voted for and supported the elected political leaders?

ELITSA: Could our collective fear that there would be no one to take responsibility for the world if we do not elect anyone be a reason why we vote for political leaders to begin with?

SOSÉ: God forbid. Whenever a human being makes a decision out of fear, such fear escalates into a deeper fear leading to insanity. We are still not taking control when we continue to believe so and this is what has kept us in a perpetual disease, isn't it?

ELITSA: What is our alternative to electing political leaders?

SOSÉ: When a human being divorces him or herself from an archetype is when that individual starts to question life, takes full responsibility, remembers to be sovereign and becomes the power that resides within. Truth frees all psychological barriers of our perceptional reality. Cease to fund and support what does not resonate with the inner being. Fund and support that which is healing our consciousness and Earth instead. It is now time to focus on and be a vital part of what is working and the positive initiatives being undertaken. "Be the change that you want to see in the world" said Mahatma Gandhi.

ELITSA: What is your opinion on geographical borders?

SOSÉ: It is a vicious circle. Fear builds borders while borders prolong the fear and the resulting division. Borders focus on separation rather than on unity. How are we supposed to find solutions to present societal and environmental challenges if political parties and human beings continuously oppose each other rather than work with each other?

It is not about focusing on enemies

threatening us. We need to walk away from the fear mode because we can prolong the path of evolution, but not avoid it. Perhaps there was a justification for the ego in the past, yet at this point, we need to connect all consciousness in order to save our planet. It is impossible to connect the cosmic energy between heaven and Earth unless we are companions with each other. We do not need guns to accomplish this. We achieve it in peace, in love. We undertake it because we know that connecting consciousness unifies rather than divides. When we unify, magic happens. Unity is a dance to harmony. When we create vastness in the universe, the very vastness itself opens a space where oppression no longer exists. Humanity cannot be unified unless all borders break down while borders fall on their own when we think universally. We can change our world swiftly within 24 hours as a collective consciousness when we no longer see separate religions, separate countries, different languages and statuses. What would the world be like if these colors didn't exist? My canvas will be quite dreary without a different color. I love the color. The color of differences is the color of sameness.

The physical bodies of all of us belong to this planet. We all have the innate right to prosperity. It is our divine sovereignty. What is called forth is political leaders all over the world and consciousness unifying to support the human race and Earth with everything that we can. The rest is just political propaganda.

ELITSA: What is mind control?

SOSÉ: An implanted veil of illusion, a root of a tree with many branches. If you are wearing a veil, unveil your veil.

ELITSA: What do some of these branches look like?

SOSÉ: When you govern large, you govern small. There are trillions of branches. One is in the form of laws. Another branch is in the form of subliminal messages, directing you to purchase a product without inquiring whether it is dangerous for humanity and the environment or to donate to a cause for artificially created problems without questioning where such funding is being directed to or such problems originating from. We funded everything with good intentions. When we start to question the truth behind such veils is when they begin to drop like petals of a flower.

ELITSA: This is so true. Having acquired marketing knowledge, I have observed how advertisements are specifically designed to portray a positive, beneficial, healthy image of a product with the use of manipulative strategies such as different colors and emotion-based triggers. The truth behind the disguise is that the product being advertised is encumbered with inorganic chemicals, harming the human being and the environment. Could this be an example of what you are referring to?

SOSÉ: This is exactly what I meant.

ELITSA: Would you say that Pavlov's classical conditioning (rewarding and punishing behavior) is another method of mind control?

SOSÉ: Yes. If you do something opposing the mind control agenda, you are punished financially, through restricting your liberties or both. On the opposite, if you support the deceit, you are rewarded through bonuses, social praise and status.

ELITSA: How are problems created and effective solutions generated?

SOSÉ: We create, facilitate and perpetuate problems by remaining focused on them. Every problem has a solution. Each solution is simple. It begins with an awareness of the truth about a problem and it proceeds with summoning up the courage to implement a solution. It is just so beautiful and powerful.

ELITSA: What is at the root of environmental problems and more specifically, how can we solve them?

SOSÉ: Environmental problems are the manifestations of human beings making choices that are not aligned with the highest good for all. To be successful in solving environmental problems, we must legalize modern technology that has been invented to free our planet.

ELITSA: Who are we as a human race?

SOSÉ: We are part of everything - part of consciousness, part of the connectedness on this planet. We are all part of that sameness, oneness, love.

ELITSA: Did we originate on Earth?

SOSÉ: This is a deep question. To simplify it, yes, everything originated on Earth, yet we are all eternal.

ELITSA: Are you suggesting that a soul can experience itself in different forms?

SOSÉ: Yes. A soul or consciousness comes on Earth in different forms of itself in order to know its spirit, in order to know its Godliness. You cannot separate soul and spirit, yet on some level it seems like they are different.

ELITSA: What is a spirit?

SOSÉ: The omnipotent presence some of us call God, some of us call the Creator, Brahma. A spirit has many names and yet one. First you experience consciousness. Then you transition into a second version of experiencing consciousness, which is the sub-consciousness before you can tap into the supra-consciousness. From consciousness to sub-consciousness to supra-consciousness, which I call the soul's journey. When we communicate, we do so from a conscious level, when we speak wisdom, we engage the subconscious level and when we meditate, we experience the supra-conscious level. Sometimes, we can embody all three, yet it is impossible to disconnect one from another. After consciousness and sub-consciousness are connected, we experience the true spirit which we call God, Creator or supra-consciousness. This is when we know our true Godliness and discover that we are that Creator, that we are that spirit.

In other words, the soul chooses to experience everything. It separates itself into duality, into understanding what it feels like to be conscious of the matrix. In the process, its awareness expands and through the very questioning of what is consciousness or who are we in relationship to that matrix, it discovers that there is a sub-consciousness which leads it to asking the question of what is sub-consciousness. We write songs, philosophies around the topic of sub-consciousness. We will do the inexhaustible to discover it. After we have experienced both consciousness and sub-consciousness, we start to question if there is more than consciousness and sub-consciousness. The "who am I" questioning leads us to knowing our Godly self which is the supra-consciousness or the integration of all consciousness and sub-consciousness. So many people talk about consciousness and sub-consciousness, yet few elaborate on supra-consciousness which I refer to as the soul integrating itself into oneness.

ELITSA: Is there consciousness beyond the supra-consciousness?

SOSÉ: *Be that and you would know.*

ELITSA: So, it appears that the more we question, the more we know and the more we know, the more there is to discover?

SOSÉ: Yes. It is infinite. The discovering of who we are is infinite.

ELITSA: What Socrates says: "The only true wisdom is in knowing you know nothing" appears to relate to such realization.

SOSÉ: The more we ask, the less we know because there is so much more to ask.

ELITSA: You mentioned that we are all eternal. How do we gain awareness of such eternity?

SOSÉ: Whenever we ask a question, we automatically jump into experiencing that question, into a form. The infinite will provide us with the answer of what we are experiencing at that moment. When we integrate that beautiful wisdom, we continue onto experiencing the next question, the next awareness of ourselves, the deeper knowing of who we are.

ELITSA: Because our experience of

questioning is eternal, it creates the perception that the knowing of ourselves is eternal, it is infinite. But how could we be certain of its infinite nature from a moment of not knowing where it is leading us to?

SOSÉ: *The secret is to dance into the unknown. Until then, we will not. It is when we are not afraid that we do not know everything, but we do want to know. The unknowingness reveals to us to the knowingness and when we realize the knowingness, we are in the unknowingness. Be in a state of unknowingness all the time. When a human being is in a state of unknowingness, creation happens. When we know everything, creation stops. When we truly live in the unknown, magic presents itself. Embrace that, do not fight it. Why should I be battling something that I should not battle? The universe and natural law is in constant impermanence in order for expansion to take place. It is when we are in that flow that it is magical. Not one moment or one day is going to be the same. It is so incredibly beautiful when we really begin to see that. We are constantly growing, changing, learning something about ourselves.*

As far as my knowingness extends, the Creator always existed, always is and always will be, expressing itself in many forms of itself.

It is in its journey to experiencing its existence. When something is omnipresent, omnipotent, it always existed. We have to experience ourselves deeper into the higher frequency to know more of its essence. As far as I know, at this moment of evolution, I always existed.

ELITSA: What does the experience of the known and the unknown look like?

SOSÉ: *I will introduce you to a metaphor to answer your question. There was a king who fell from an apple tree and became dreadfully ill as a result of the fall. The news that the king was in bed due to a fall from an apple tree was publicized. People sent healing and gifts to the king. Everyone who was concerned about the king's well-being surrounded his castle to assist him, to heal him. He would not let anyone inside his castle. He gave a speech to the people who came to see him and thanked them profusely for assisting him. He stated that he has one request – to search for another human being who has experienced the same as himself, someone who has fallen from an apple tree. So people finally found a very poor old man who lived by himself in the village. He had fallen from an apple tree and was ill for years from the fall. The man knocked on the door of the castle and said to the king: "I have fallen from an* *apple tree and I am here to visit you". The king opened the door to the man and welcomed him inside. The king knew that the only person who has experienced the pains associated with falling from an apple tree was the one who has himself or herself fallen from an apple tree. The theory behind this metaphor is that we do not know the unknown unless we experience that which we do not know.*

ELITSA: If creation is characterized by its infinite nature, the purpose of life then seems to be to simply experience ourselves through life?

SOSÉ: Yes.

ELITSA: This implies that every time we take another life away, we are depriving that soul from its innate right to experience itself in the form, time and place it seeks to experience itself as? We are literally interrupting that person's evolution, violating the free will of that soul, imposing our own path onto his or her own?

SOSÉ: Yes.

ELITSA: Life itself implies a being living

and experiencing itself. Death implies the ceasing of creation. So, if we value life, yet we take away life, we must live in the illusion of appreciating life. In fact, we value death. Otherwise, we would not take another person's life for absolutely no apparent reason. So, we must decide, do we value life or do we value death, do we value creation and evolution or destruction?

SOSÉ: *Yes. When we take another life away, we are short-cutting the circuit of that soul, depriving it from the opportunity to experience itself on Earth. We are interfering with its free will. By taking that life, we are literally breaking the contract of the free will. We can delve even further and expand to life and death in general.*

There is so much to death and the fear around it. There are people who are petrified of death, of dying. Why? Why not accept it as a part of life? Besides, it is just stepping from one beautiful passage-way into another to experience ourselves into a different version of the self. We step into these unknowns that we fear so much. Why not be glad to experience another unknown? Most human beings feel that when they die, life ends so they would literally create that end for themselves. Death is just an illusion we create as a result of the fear of stepping into the unknown. Every human being is going to experience death on a different level. Some people who have died and awoken from death report seeing themselves going through a tunnel of light, having a family or a friend come to help them transition into a new reality, a different experience of the soul on its journey.

ELITSA: What happens to that person we cut the circuits of?

SOSÉ: The violated person is going to experience him or herself as he or she was originally intended to experience him or herself as. The challenge remains with the individual who took that free will away. Such challenge is embedded within the law of the universe called cause and effect.

ELITSA: When we murder another, our life is taken away, which causes us to learn to abstain from killing?

SOSÉ: Yes. This allows us to experience what that felt like. It is not bad or good. We understand that when we cause something, it comes back to us. When we understand cause and effect, we understand the soul's journey. When we pour love through our hearts, we receive it back. When we kill elephants, as another example, and thus remove this beautiful frequency from Earth, such an act leaves us living without it so now we experience that.

ELITSA: More specifically, how does the desecrated soul experience that violation of free will? What happens to his or her soul journey upon death? How does this type of death affect that soul, that person?

SOSÉ: Such type of death drastically affects the individual as his or her free will was taken away. He or she experiences deep pain and confusion as he or she is leaving the body as the murder was unexpected. That person can transition to being a ghost, a poltergeist, afraid to exit our dimensional reality, re-living the traumatic experience over and over as the death was unexpected, leaving the soul deprived of the opportunity to experience itself while it was on Earth. It takes that soul a while to shift its consciousness to a state where it seeks to experience itself as beauty again. The person will eventually continue on his or her soul journey.

ELITSA: To recap, the ghost that remains in our dimensional space does so because it hasn't completed its mission on Earth so it is trying to experience it without its body which leaves it confused as now it has no body to experience itself with, yet it still seeks the experience for which it came?

SOSÉ: Yes, and that I also refer to as cause and effect.

ELITSA: And what would it take for that ghost to transition back into a body to continue on its journey or rather to experience that which it never could because its life was taken away?

SOSÉ: Since we are completely connected, the person who took that soul away has to confess for his or her actions. He or she needs to confront him or herself for what he or she has done (not deny it or live in guilt), literally confront the soul he or she took the life away from, ask for forgiveness from that soul and free it. Truly, the person who caused the pain can free that soul. When we take a soul away, we take the free will of that soul upon ourselves. It is now our responsibility to free it as the murder prevented that soul's growth. It is cause and effect and it is the same as paying karmic debt. Everything in the Universe moves in a circular motion. Whenever we have caused some sort of an effect, honestly, the only thing we can do to balance that energy is through forgiveness.

ELITSA: Can the violated person, with his or her own free will, choose to free him or herself alone or does he or she always have to wait for the perpetrator to free him or her and to forgive him or herself for the violence?

SOSÉ: *Yes, the infringed upon soul can also free itself and take its essence and soul back by forgiving the person who caused the pain as he or she did not have access to higher awareness at the moment he or she took that person's life away. So sometimes the person who had his or her free will affected can be more evolved than the person who compromised his or her life. We can explore that topic even further. When a soul recognizes its higher state of consciousness and knows its higher planes of existence, sometimes it will actually bring such a situation upon itself so it can experience that part of the self and strengthen the soul.*

ELITSA: What do you mean by strengthening the soul?

SOSÉ: *There is no wrong or right to any experience and to being murdered in particular.*

We choose such experiences in order for us to understand, to grow, for the soul to know itself. Ultimately, it is about searching for the light and light cannot know itself as light; it has to be through contrast. So, there is no such a phenomenon as a definite answer. To break away from the wheel of rebirth is to look at an experience deeply. Choosing not to do so is what propels us to remain into a state of rebirth. In order to exit this wheel is to know that such an experience was initially actually created by us to experience that so-called dark, that contrast, that duality, no matter how it manifested itself, whether through manipulation, mind control, murder. The soul of the desecrated person perpetuated that to experience it, to see what it is like.

ELITSA: So it comes down to forgiveness - either the perpetrator forgiving the violated person, the infringed upon individual forgiving the perpetrator or both in order for the desecrated soul to free itself and in order for the perpetrator to be free once he or she has forgiven himself or herself for his or her action?

SOSÉ: Yes.

ELITSA: If a person actually wanted to

experience sudden, unjustified death and yet he or she is undergoing dramatic experiences as a ghost instead of rejoicing with that specific part of his or her journey, would this imply that, while being a ghost, the violated person may not be consciously aware of his or her deeper choice to experience such drastic death? Would this then suggest that we have many levels or dimensions to ourselves and we may not be aware of some of them on a conscious level?

SOSÉ: Yes.

ELITSA: Experiencing ourselves in different facets of existence in order to know the difference?

SOSÉ: Yes.

ELITSA: And with every experience of difference, the deeper we delve into that unknown, into that light, into knowing who we are?

SOSÉ: Yes.

ELITSA: And could we also delve deeper through preference rather than always through difference?

SOSÉ: You are always creating so you are choosing every moment of your life through preferences. So yes, what is your preference since you are the creator of all, what are you choosing to be at that moment?

ELITSA: So preference is actually difference. It is in effect contrast because one preference automatically excludes all other possibilities.

SOSÉ: When we choose to experience ourselves into different aspects of ourselves, when we start journeying inward, sometimes we fail to look at the experience, we become so entangled in our creation that we forget to monitor ourselves. "How is this experience making me feel?" Thought and feelings create our experiences. In order to not choose to experience the opposite of ourselves, we begin to monitor our thoughts and feelings. This is when we become more conscious of the law of cause and effect.

ELITSA: So, it comes down to choice - do we choose to experience ourselves as the opposite of who we innately are or as love? Both are okay and both fall under the law of cause and effect?

SOSÉ: Correct, because at the end it is about the experience itself. Consciously the human being inflicting the pain is not being aware of what is taking place. Such awareness resides in the subconscious. It is in the heart, in the mind, in the DNA. He or she has to take responsibility for himself or herself for creating his or her own reality. It is when we take total responsibility for creating our reality that we would completely understand the law of cause and effect.

ELITSA: So, through darkness, the person inflicting the pain comes to know light and hence the process of evolution, of going deeper into ourselves and knowing ourselves as that connectedness and oneness, as God?

SOSÉ: Yes. You could choose to call it darkness or you could choose to experience the other side of God. If you continue to see it as darkness, that same principle of darkness will play itself out as darkness. What we are afraid of is not the dark. How can we be afraid of the dark when the dark is afraid of us, which is the reason why it seeks our demise? What we are absolutely petrified of is our Godliness, our grandness. We chose that darkness with love. We just became lost in the illusion of that love.

There is something more powerful than how we view our world. A soul has a history. It is on this reincarnation wheel to learn the library of itself. So, every piece of darkness that we experienced was nothing more than the highest blessing. Every piece of it, no matter how hard it seemed the moment that we were going through it, allowed us to know more of our beautiful selves. Darkness changes the meaning when you see it as a contrast. Otherwise, it continues on the wheel of karmic debt.

Life is exciting, illuminating. It is truly magical. When we step into its magic, we see the beauty of our darkness. Then we truly see the beauty that we were and are through that darkness. Once an individual understands the higher states of consciousness, the lessons one has to learn will cultivate character. He or she will understand him or herself, the knowing of the soul self. What makes Sosé, Sosé? If I was pure light, I would not be talking to you, I will be pure light. But because I am Sosé and you are Elitsia, it helps to develop this beautiful character. When you develop such character, it makes you stronger, your personality is defined, the light and love that you are becomes transparent. Because now you understand the difference, you had learned it. Imagine if you always lived in light, what would such an experience be like? The experience of the soul journey is so beautiful because we take our pure light soul and building a character to it.

ELITSA: So, the only way to experience ourselves as light and love is to choose to be that through preference, not through destroying the darkness?

SOSÉ: It is not about destroying the darkness. It is about balancing. There is no darkness to destroy. Once we arrive at the conclusion that there is not really any darkness even if to us it seems as such, it becomes a dance. We cannot fight darkness with dark. This is where we are going to find peace – in supporting what works for us.

ELITSA: Besides building a character and a library of experiences, why else would a soul choose to experience the difference of itself?

SOSÉ: It chooses it because it wants to free itself. Tibetans teach not to attach to an experience. Attachment is founded on the basis of an electron spin and has a cause and effect property. It creates a karmic wheel which propels us to continue re-creating the experience we became attached to. The mind compares itself with the other or to the event of its own life. It creates belief systems and becomes attached to them. Attachment is represented by many forms. For example, if someone tells you that you are ugly, you attach to that judgment and create a karmic wheel, which causes you to be reborn to experience light without attaching yourself to that cause. The heart makes the choice to break the chains of re-birthing and reincarnation. Once we understand not to attach, that of itself brings visibility to the mind and allows it integrate the current situation, the problem.

ELITSA: So, each experience either allows us to or prevents us from realizing our innate light on a deeper level?

SOSÉ: Yes.

ELITSA: When a soul knows itself as light, what it is not aware of at such a moment of knowing is that there is light even deeper than the light it is at present? And it is the choice to experience something different that allows it to achieve higher states of its own existence and to delve into even deeper dimensions of its pureness as light?

SOSÉ: Right. The purpose of the soul is to conquer the mind and the emotion. Acquiring self-love is truly the only way to accomplish that.

ELITSA: But earlier you mentioned that it is through thought and feelings that we create our reality. Could you tell us more about thought, emotion and the heart?

SOSÉ: Thought (mind) and emotion (heart) are interconnected. We create through thought and emotion so it is through there that we come to know ourselves as who we are, create utopia in our inner being and on this planet. When we see ourselves as harmful thoughts and emotions, we are going to destroy ourselves and everything around us because we are all interconnected.

Once we gain pure mind and heart on a conscious and sub-conscious level, we may choose to delve further into the unknown, experiencing the connection between the divine mind and heart, which is the supra-consciousness or God. It is impossible to define the experience of divine mind and heart as it is an experience of oneness, of omnipresent, omnipotent state of bliss devoid of third-dimensional thought and emotion.

ELITSA: Through said experiences, we realize that the negative, destructiveness is not who we are which causes us to choose to experience ourselves as light and love?

SOSÉ: Yes. When we are aware of our tests, lessons, experiences, we realize that we have been reincarnated on Earth to learn such lessons. These are opportunities for the soul to advance. It is about the actions that we choose upon such awareness, the vibrations that we decide to emanate – love or destruction-based. Anything that we give our energy to, that energy will multiply. The question is how adept are we at controlling our minds and hearts not to focus on darkness, but to instead focus on the present moment, on the now, bringing the soul into that now moment, learning to connect our pure mind and heart.

ELITSA: Such an awareness and intent will free us from the lower dimensions and shift us to our higher self? Dis-attachment and being at the present moment?

SOSÉ: Yes. The experience causing the attachment will continue to project itself until we learn not to attach to it. It is really about learning about who we are.

ELITSA: What does the experience of ourselves as light and love look like now that we know how the opposite of that is manifested?

SOSÉ: Experience it and you will know. More specifically, we recognize it when our soul remains in balance between the feminine and masculine aspects of itself, the yin and yang. We recognize it when we meet another individual different than us, with opinions, religion, country, ethnicity, background, expression of the mental, emotional and spiritual essence other than ours and we are absolutely accepting and loving of that individual. It is when we become spiritually aware of these differences, see them in our inner being and accept them as sameness, as one, not as polarity. The dance is in those differences.

It is not about changing someone else, but rather about mastering ourselves, our thoughts and emotions, bringing ourselves into a state of oneness, total Godliness. God is oneness manifesting itself in different aspects of itself. We arrive at the conclusion that everything we have searched for is within ourselves.

ELITSA: Letting go of attachment and duality and embracing self-awareness and mastery?

SOSÉ: *Exactly.*

ELITSA: Could you tell us about the manifestations of love in our present day?

SOSÉ: *Look around you. You can see the manifestation of love and light everywhere. We identified love as: "I will do this for you under the condition that you do something back for me." There are so many different manifestations of what we created through love. We would write poetry, love stories around it and yet we also manipulated it in order to fit it into the perfect worldview that we created. We saw it with our impure minds and hearts in order for us to gain something back. That then led us into attachment, sorrow, little us, compartments. When love is love. Love does not have compartments; it is unity, peace and joy. Love is powerful - it forgives, purifies and connects.*

ELITSA: What are more specifically the qualities of love?

SOSÉ: *Be that and you would know.*

ELITSA: What is the opposite of love?

SOSÉ: Fear. The energy of fear was created as an illusion. The whole planet is being affected when a political leader or any other human being, indifferently of status, number of academic degrees and credentials, makes a decision out of fear and not from a place of love. Fear gives birth to greed. Instead of admitting to such a mistake, the ego mind would do everything in its power to cover the illusion-based decision due to yet another fear of being punished. It is now a matter of coming forward and admitting to the truth so a solution can be devised for a particular challenge. It is more important not to focus on wrong decisions and pointing fingers, but rather on solutions to such obstacles, on collectively taking responsibility as we are all actors in the play.

ELITSA: Can love and fear co-exist?

SOSÉ: Two vibrationally-opposing energies cannot exist at the same moment.

ELITSA: While we consider children as these little beings who know nothing about life, it appears that they are our greatest masters as they are full of love. We tend to project our own fears and insecurities into them instead of allowing them to project their love onto us.

SOSÉ: A child already comes with worldly wisdom and pure divine love. It is about allowing that child now to express its own wisdom-ness without any outside interference and then support such expression.

ELITSA: Besides expressing itself through us, what else does God express itself through?

SOSÉ: God is in a flower. God is in the tree. God is in the ocean. God is in the rains. God is in the forests. God is in the wild. God is that vegetable that feeds us. God is that sun that gives us sunshine. God is that moon that shines at night. God is the stars. It is endless what God is. God is everywhere and in everything. God is nothing but love.

ELITSA: How more specifically does each individual's vibrational state influence the world we live in?

SOSÉ: Such process can be equated to a circular motion. Circles are in everything – in plants, animals, in the sun and the moon. We judge everything that we observe when we are in a state of low vibration. Such frequency carries a negative charge. When we are upset, such state disconnects us from our natural rhythm, from the experience of the moment, of oneness. The heart's natural rhythm is compromised. When we stop this natural flow, we experience ourselves in a low vibration because we are part of that rhythm of nature, the rhythm of creation. When we break the rhythm, we say that we are not worthy. When we say that there are crimes in the world, we are not elevating this word; we are breaking the very rhythm of it. When we are projecting suffering, it is out of rhythm. When we keep repeating it, we are focusing on the suffering of the world and such frequency projects outwardly. When we continuously communicate war, the frequency would not move into a higher level because it is breaking the rhythm of nature.

When we transition our attention from low-vibrational states of being to love, we align with the natural rhythm of creation and our self-worth is revealed. The world around us changes as a result. Instead of sending the intent and observing that there is a child starving in Africa, we change this rhythm in our hearts and minds and see that this child is full of abundance. Such aligned with the natural rhythm perception projects outward. We have just shifted the rhythm of the child and the world we want to experience. When everyone vibrates in joy, love, abundance, we are connecting to that natural rhythm so our world swiftly changes. We would be in the rhythm of abundance, in the rhythm of the moment, not yesterday, not tomorrow.

Step away from the world's bondage. See it as a free world, not a bondage world. When we become so bounded to our attachments, we lose the sense of self and then we are easily swayed back and forth, like a pendulum of a clock. The question should be asked: "What is my relationship to my world, to my planet, to my creation all around me"? We would see that the very question of it will bring us right back to our truthfulness. If our relationship is to harm someone, then it is a world of harm. If it is to love, that is what will be present into our world. Once we are aware of the difference, we will not have to afflict pain onto ourselves or others as we realize that living in this perpetual guilt causes suffering. But many of us live in duality. We are pulling and tugging. We judge everything; we are in the state of pointing fingers, not in the state of seeing the abundance on the planet. The manifestation of this rhythm is massive. We are great beings who have done great things with good intentions, but somehow we stopped questioning who we are and that is what truly happened.

It is so easy to be in the rhythm of nature. We can close our eyes and feel the rhythm of the heart, the self, the connection with this oneness. This is when we are in a perfect rhythm. The problems of today, yesterday and tomorrow completely disappear. Look in the mirror and ask yourself: "Who am I?" "Am I this victim or am I this powerful God or Goddess?" And just by asking this question, you feel that vibration in your body when your whole skin turns upside down and speaks loud to you: "Yes, you are God." Merge into it, bounce into it, sense it, smell it, make love to it. So next time you look in the mirror, you do not see the reflection of the little me because it doesn't exist; it is just an illusion. The you who is inside of yourself is so grand, it is so infinite that it would be impossible for any poet or any philosopher to articulate the essence and the beauty of it.

When we gain pure mind and heart, the world becomes a phenomenal world, in a perfect rhythm and realization. When we stay with the inner journey, we become the magicians of our minds and hearts. Then we become the magicians of nature and everything around us because we articulate the life of perfection, we see perfection in all.

ELITSA: How do you interpret psychological problems?

SOSÉ: *We search outside of ourselves for a professional mental health therapist to answer* *the questions which reside within ourselves. Yet, psychologists and psychiatrists are still themselves researching the answers to such questions. We go as far as to sedate ourselves with medications as a means to escape confronting the energies that need to be transmuted in our inner being. We tend to avoid alternative healing methods which are effective as we may not yet be ready to heal or because created systems do not support such methods. We delved a little bit more into the realm of so-called darkness because it was more convenient for us to do so.*

ELITSA: What happens with that free space when we do not love ourselves completely, when we are fragmented? Can a dark energy frequency implant itself artificially to fill that space or does it remain numb or empty until we fully embody love?

SOSÉ: Everything on this planet, no matter how dark it may appear to be, can heal through love. Love can heal everything that has been artificially projected into our being and move galaxies, never mind mountains. Dark energies do not stand a chance when we are in our power because that is when we are one with the primordial frequency of divinity, one with all of life.

ELITSA: Is it possible to confuse that artificial dark implant with who we are innately and how do we remember who we are if so?

SOSÉ: By being constantly the watcher of thoughts and emotions. When we bring the mind and heart into the divine is when we would know. All our lives, we have known that we are God. Yet, we created an illusion, a box, a compartmentalization, a manifestation. We cannot raise our consciousness unless we confront such illusions, open these manifestations, metaphysical compartments that we created for ourselves. From the perspective of the moment, we say: "Oh my God, it isn't so; I was just not thinking right." A soul cannot evolve unless it heals its past. How did that compartment rose and how did we make sure that it was locked, on a shelf, forgotten about while at the same time it persisted to play out in the background? We continued to be reminded of that box.

    We have to start somewhere. It is about looking at our past. Instead of pointing fingers at yourself, open the box and see that the illusion is not true. It is just an archetype that you kept alive on your shelf. This is not who you are, you have never been that. Implants are a form of repeated recordings: "My mother abandoned me when I was 5." You are 60 years old now and still repeating the same record. Yet, now you see that your mother had more boxes than you did, more manifestations of an illusion than you did. This is why loving ourselves and freeing boxes is so important. Illusions are nothing but Maya, the greatest deceiver. When you choose to look at such compartments is when you start healing. In turn, since you know the truth, you are going to heal your mother, heal everybody because now you know the difference.

Blaming another human being is the largest disease on this planet. It is reckless. When it starts to spread, it creates commotion on the psyche of a human being because you are constantly telling yourself that you are the little you.

I will give you an example. Moses's mother gave birth to Moses, yet a tragedy took place in his mother's environment where the so-called dark forces were killing all of the boys. The mother had two choices - either she held onto her child or found safety for him. So, she wrapped Moses and placed him on a boat sailing towards Egypt. As an adult, Moses discovered that he was adopted. He did not blame his mother for abandoning him. Rather, he searched for the truth and discovered that his mother did everything in her power to save him from the dark forces. He took his power back and he freed all the men who were enslaved by the dark forces.

ELITSA: So, we heal implants when we realize that the frequency of the implant does not resonate with our inner being, which drives us to become or remember the opposite of that?

SOSÉ: Something that does not resonate with our inner being cannot survive there very long. An illusion disappears when we identify it. We just have to be aware of it. It is impossible to sway into the projected illusionary world when we monitor ourselves. When we are constantly focusing on the illusion, that becomes large, we are feeding that ego, the demon, with lunches and delicious dinner. We are giving it the best.

ELITSA: What do the so-called demons want to achieve, what is their intent?

SOSÉ: To project themselves onto us so we can see that we are more than that. When we attach ourselves to it, we focus on the negative, feeding it gourmet food.

ELITSA: What do you mean by feeding it? What is that creating?

SOSÉ: A separation between us and the divine. When we see that it is an illusion, it cannot cause harm unless we give it our free will to do so. When we are taking the beautiful energy into that darkness, then the dark energy would become bigger. We learn not to give the power to the contrary of ourselves. Darkness is a teacher. It is going to come to a point when we do not need a teacher any longer. Teachers disappear; we are masters now. We no longer search for a teacher outside of ourselves. It stops.

ELITSA: What else can we do to re-connect to light and love, to the source of divine energy?

SOSÉ: Project light, love, compassion. It is that simple. When you see war, do not see it as war, see it as peace. When you see starvation, do not see it as starvation, see it as abundance. It is all in the perception: perceiving and projecting the little self or the joy and the divinely self. Supreme love and illumination can only exist when you connect with the supra-consciousness. It is a dreamless state, a candle that never burns down. When you are that, you can fill all creation with light. You are that light bulb that moves even faster than the speed of thought. It is an inexhaustible resource. You can see all the illusion-based manifestations that were created. All compartmentalization disappears.

ELITSA: What is the purpose of sexual energy and why is it being misused? Its misuse appears to be epidemic. Why is it detrimental when it is misused or imposed on someone?

SOSÉ: Sexual energy is what created all life on this planet. Anything that is created and expanded is derived from sex. It is a totally natural state of being. Everything on Earth has male and female energy so whether it is a species or a human, it is sexually connected in order to continue the process of creation. The very sexuality is the transcendental principle of attributes of the formless God, it is the instrument, the music of the divine. Think about when interconnected with that energy, in that moment, how deep we are in deep bliss. We even cry out: "Oh God." Our sexuality is manifested when we are in a state of bliss, in a state of somati. It is the cosmic wheel of life, the ultimate union between the physical, the consciousness, sub-consciousness and supra-

consciousness and it is the most sacred. No human being can describe its sacredness because that is the ultimate manifestation of the oneness.

The largest problem on our planet is sexuality. Sexual energy is being abused and exploited because it is the highest form of intervening with our divine self. Nothing else can be more powerful than that. Sexual energy is impermanent so when it is compromised, the frequency of the natural rhythm changes. When abused, it disconnects us from the flow, from the rhythm of the universe. It prolongs the knowing of our divinity. When the stage of sexuality is interrupted, it compromises the very state of bliss and somati. Manipulating sacredness is worse than causing a murder. Because this is the discharge of liquid golden light, the being undergoes drastic, unveiling, conscious, sub-consciousness, supra-consciousness experiences and it takes one a long time to come to understand the laws of the universe. It is the most devastating state of the soul because sexual energy is part of the rhythm of creation.

ELITSA: So, in a natural rhythm every being chooses their sexual experiences and anything opposing to that free will is breaking universal laws.

SOSÉ: Yes. It disconnects us from that natural rhythm because universal laws have been broken. We realize now that we can go back to that connection rather than seeing it as us being disconnected from that natural state. We can connect again with the natural flow. Whatever we perceive will be so – whether connection or disconnection. The abuse can manipulate the body, but it cannot manipulate the soul.

ELITSA: Why do sexual offenders perceive that it is okay to abuse others and don't see the harm they are inflicting on those they abuse?

SOSÉ: Because they themselves have experienced such. If they saw the cause, they would not be in that state of inflicting that very cause. Great masters say: "God forgive them for they do not know what they do." Instead of healing, the abusive experience is constantly being projected outside. The manifestation of cause and effect is the manifestation of a sex offender. Sexual offenders who have themselves been sexually abused are in constant playing-it-out scenario. That then projects itself onto another so this is a huge call for help.

We judge it instead of seeing that the person is really crying out for help. This is a human being in deep pain because the sexual abuse has been inflicted upon that individual. The very essence of that person has been taken away. It took away the imagination, the trust. Someone took that beauty out of that person and left him or her stripped out of his or her dignity. He or she completely loses trust especially when this happened by a family member when that individual was a child. Once that happens to that child, it remains with him or her. He or she continues to choose abusive relationships because he or she cannot transcend beyond what has been done to him or her.

So then, what do we do as a society to sex offenders? We point fingers, we put them in jail: "Let's punish him or her" and we label that person, which adds more distress. The very essence of sacredness has been taken and judged instead of seeing it for what it is and bringing compassion and healing, making sure that this individual lets go of the guilt, fear and self-blame that he or she caused the abuse inflicted upon him or herself.

This is why we have so called psychologists, psychiatrists, healers on this world. Sexually abusive individuals go for treatment for years and years and still do not heal as therapists are seeing such patients subjectively, not objectively. They are projecting their judgment-filled feelings onto their patients. Successful treatment depends on the therapist; is he or she viewing the patient as another human being or accusing him or her? That patient would feel the difference. There is a tremendous amount of trust that needs to be gained in order for that individual to be healed because the experience was so drastic. The patient has to be treated with extreme compassion. The taking of your innocence as a child really affects you deeply. You have to heal the child, not the adult. Until then, the scenario will continue to play itself out. Psychoanalysts with expertise in hypnosis are the most suited therapists to provide healing for sexual offenders.

ELITSA: Is their behavior justified because they have been through such experience themselves?

SOSÉ: No. It is about how are we seeing it, how are we justifying that.

ELITSA: What prevents those who do not have self-control to abstain from abusing another?

SOSÉ: Some sexual offenders do have self-control; they are jumping right back into that rhythm. Yet, this is not always the case. Look at our pedophilia world. It is everywhere. Our own governments are involved with it. Sex offenders who are not able to exert self-control are in deep pain. Their minds are overly clouded. They live with the abuse inflicted upon themselves day in and day out. It is a vibration. They keep projecting that scenario. They know that what they are acting upon is not resonating, but it is that reliving of the experience that causes them to commit the abuse. They are not really aware of what they are doing. The mind slips when something like that happens. It affects the mind so badly. It has a crack; it splits the personality. That person is not totally aware as to whether he or she is the child or the 40 or 70-year-old perpetrator. The split is completely confusing.

ELITSA: When they are acting upon abusing a child, for example, they see both the child they are abusing and their perpetrator as themselves?

SOSÉ: Yes.

ELITSA: What is your opinion on marriage?

SOSÉ: Remove the conditioning and replace it with sacredness.

ELITSA: You mentioned earlier universal

laws. Who created universal laws?

SOSÉ: We did.

ELITSA: When and how?

SOSÉ: When we were omnipresent, the God particle. We created them, but we do not remember. The question should be what law do I choose to experience at the moment?

ELITSA: Can we remove old laws or add new universal laws?

SOSÉ: Nothing in this universe is about removing it. It is about what we are going to focus now on creating new. We cannot change something that has been created. The point is not to give it our power. We change the rhythm by focusing on the energy that we want to see in our world.

ELITSA: Does this mean that we can create new laws?

SOSÉ: We can remain in a state of oneness where all laws are in a state of oneness.

ELITSA: What will happen once we integrate all the laws and become the law of one?

SOSÉ: Then we would experience a total utopia.

ELITSA: And what happens next?

SOSÉ: When we arrive to that destination, we would know.

ELITSA: What was the purpose of creating universal laws?

SOSÉ: So that the soul can experience itself in different versions of itself.

ELITSA: What does an ideal, utopic world look like?

SOSÉ: An ideal world is where there is peace, unity, sovereignty, where fear is replaced with joy, abundance and love, bringing harmony into consciousness and nature. It is when we connect to the universal consciousness and bring heaven to earth; when we start seeing ourselves as divine.

As sovereign beings, when we follow the laws of nature, benevolence is evident and imminent. Gaia is already clothed in richness. It does not seek a fortune and self-gratification. It knows its completeness. A tree does not say: "Look at how magnificent I am; I provide oxygen for your lungs." Gaia does not separate between her children, but it feeds us all.

The seed of God is in all of us. God is in everyone and in everything. With love in our hearts and minds we move to the heights of morality and extend leadership to pure sincerity. We can support each other and unify our vision in harmony, clarity, love, peace and creativity. When the seed of God blossoms in us, we are all speaking the same truth, connecting our noble masculine and feminine essence. Our God nature connects us to the principle of oneness where worries, fear, manipulation and demise no longer exist.

We are now seeing and breathing the light, exhaling darkness, embracing our hearts and freeing our spirits. It is all about becoming the light, becoming that which we want to see in the world, supporting that in every possible way that we can. Make it a beautiful dance, in harmony, peace and in love and not by force. We are in the process of transcending the world. We are under contemplation and this is a fine place to be. If we passionately inspire each other with a vision, focus and determination, this will fill our bellies with full potential. We are going to wrap ourselves in this beautiful blanket, not of fear because we know that fear produced anxiety, oppressiveness, loss of spirit. It is to fully embrace, to fully know the truth of who we are. Truth without responsibility cannot exist; they are the twins of the soul.

That is so powerful and beautiful. We are looking into the truth, seeing it, we are taking responsibility, taking back our Godliness, the part of creative Godliness to not be afraid to say: "Yes, I am God." This whole planet Universe was created by us and it took extraordinary imagination to do that. That is what happens with particles of God. We did it. And now we are going to create beauty, health, imaginations, science, technologies that we would use to find solutions everywhere on this planet. Why not? Did we not have all this technology to create the opposite? Now we can create something beautiful with it. We are going to clean our oceans, allow our wildlife to run free. We are going to swim in clean oceans. We are going to eat food that is not poisoned, drink water that does not affect our minds. 99% is a superpower. We are going to look and see where we gave our power away and we are going to take responsibility. This is how we are going to heal our minds, bodies, souls, spirits. Do we have a choice? I think not. As far as I know, there is only one Gaia that feeds everybody. If you have found another one, send me a ticket. I would like to come and visit.

Instead of supporting that which does not work and has not worked for years, care for this planet because this is where our clothing is, this is where our food and houses come from, this is where everything that we experience and everything in day to day life comes from.

ELITSA: How do you view Earth?

SOSÉ: My Mother is a jewel and a fabulous mandala. She provides shelter when I am cold, food when I am hungry, water when I am thirsty. She is my temple, my candle, my perfume, my dance, my joy, my mantra. She provides me with empty space where I can play with my perception. She is an artistic beauty with mountains so high. She is my connection to my imagination, my truth. She is all and more. The gifts that she gives to me are the gifts she gives to all infinitely. Your love is endless. Thank you, Mother Earth.

ELITSA: To briefly summarize, while universal laws contribute to the evolution or expansion of consciousness, human-created laws are specifically devised to limit the creative source, the expression of the omnipresent, omnipotent soul that we all embody for purposes of generating profit and being in power. If we are to survive as a human race, we must question the truth, unify as a collective consciousness and implement effective solutions that will heal Earth - our galactic home, which provides all that is needed for us to thrive in this world. In order to experience ourselves as God, as supra-consciousness, we ought to transcend the limitations of the mind and emotion. To do so, we must question who we truly are, cease to attach to our experiences, confront our sub-conscious mind, re-connect to the energy of light, love, peace, joy, abundance, compassion, project beauty and delve into the realm of the unknown. Have I understood the essence of such universal wisdom correctly?

SOSÉ: *Yes.*

ABOUT THE AUTHORS

Sosé Gjelaj was born in Montenegro. She relocated to the United States with her family in 1969 and has lived in America since then. Sosé is an author, a philanthropist, a published poet and a pronoun artist who had spent a lifetime studying Eastern and Western philosophy. She has academic background in Arts and is the owner of "Sosé Art Gallery" located in Bennington, VT. Sosé is the founder of the "Source of Visibility," a not-for-profit humanitarian and environmental organization.

Elitsa Teneva was born in Bulgaria. She moved to the United States when she was 18 to pursue an academic career in the fields of psychology and school psychology. She graduated with a B.S. in Psychology and a minor in Child Development from Southern Vermont College in Bennington, VT, and M.Ed. with a concentration in School Psychology from the University of Massachusetts Amherst, Amherst, MA. Elitsa is a member on the Board of Directors of the "Source of Visibility."

OTHER BOOKS BY THE AUTHORS

SOVEREIGN TERRA by Sosé Gjelaj and Elitsa Teneva

Based on a theory devised by Sosé Gjelaj and with the support of 445 peer-reviewed scientific articles, "Sovereign Terra" takes a revolutionary perspective on the state of humanity and the environment and the root cause of human disease and environmental degradation. Human and environmental deterioration are the product of a secretive agenda designed by governmental and industrial enterprises to acquire absolute profit and power at the expense of human life and environmental wellness. While humanity is deceived to believe that all care is taken by key officials to ameliorate the ever-accelerating human and environmental destruction, in truth, all planning and action is undertaken to destruct the human race and Earth. Humanity and Earth are on the verge of grand-scale collapse whether manifested through environmental disaster, human disease outbreaks or the combination of both.

      We can no longer depend on those we elect to save us and our environment if we are to thrive and ensure that future generations breathe fresh air, drink clean water and consume food free of chemicals. We must act now and take full responsibility for ourselves and our planetary home. The longer we delay the implementation of restorative interventions, the more severely we will experience the devastating consequences of escalating deterioration. The first step to healing ourselves and Earth is awareness, the grand awakening to the truth. "Sovereign Terra" opens the eyes to the visibly invisible so we can, individually

and collectively, consciously take action,
save ourselves and Earth.

NOUN=VERB by Sosé Gjelaj and Elitsa Teneva

Based on over 250 research articles, Noun=Verb explores the fundamental reasons for the staggering rates of psychological disorders, violence, incarceration, failure to graduate, unemployment, suicide and exploitation among humanity. Findings demonstrate that maladjustment and trauma are not accidental. Rather, such events are deliberately orchestrated by various governmental sectors (i.e. educational system; public and mental health; judicial system) relying on an array of harmful methods (i.e. fear appeals; punishment). The goal is the acquisition of absolute corporate profit at the expense of life. Solving the injustice would require awareness and the courage to cultivate and implement a value system founded on spirituality (i.e., focus on creativity; love; autonomy; reaching one's maximum potential; positive emotions) and not on self-serving corporate interest.

THE 13ᵀᴴ SECRET CODE by Sosé Gjelaj

The 13th Secret Code is a compilation of selected poems written by Sosé Gjelaj in the past almost five decades. Sosé's wisdom and creativity flow through the pages as the reader delves into the ocean of source energy and the experiences of our eternal soul. Love, the evolution of human consciousness and the unknown are some of the topics that Sosé explores through her artistic pen. The reader is gifted with a masterpiece of mystery and magic.

www.ingramcontent.com/pod-product-compliance
Lightning Source LLC
Chambersburg PA
CBHW061250040426
42444CB00010B/2327